Original title:
Living the Dream, Loving You

Copyright © 2024 Creative Arts Management OÜ
All rights reserved.

Author: Christopher White
ISBN HARDBACK: 978-9908-0-1282-7
ISBN PAPERBACK: 978-9908-0-1283-4

Infinite Horizons

In a world where socks don't match,
We dance like fools without a catch,
Chasing rainbows in the sky,
With silly grins, we'll fly so high.

The coffee's cold, but hearts are warm,
In pajamas, we create our charm,
With every laugh, a story spins,
Together, oh, where shall we begin?

Radiance in Every Word

Whispers sweet like honey bees,
We giggle under swaying trees,
Each silly pun, a perfect art,
You're the sunshine in my heart.

From awkward dances in the rain,
To finding joy in all the mundane,
Your laughter rings, a melody,
Among the chaos, it's just you and me.

The Bridge of Us

We build our dreams with silly blocks,
And wear our hearts like mismatched socks,
In every blunder, love prevails,
With our ship sailing on whimsy sails.

With every wink, we craft a tale,
Adventures bright that never pale,
You and I, a journey grand,
Side by side, we take a stand.

A Garden in Bloom

In a garden full of giggles and cheer,
We plant our love, year after year,
With every sprout, a funny quirk,
In this soil, happiness works.

We'll dance with daisies, twirl with glee,
As butterflies laugh at you and me,
In this patch of joy, we'll forever stay,
Where every moment is a sunny day.

Dreamweavers of Our Story

In the kitchen, we dance with pots,
Your moves are wild, and I forget the thoughts.
Spinning around, we spill the flour,
Laughter erupts, oh, what a power.

Our story's ink is a little smudged,
With each little quirk, we become budged.
You steal my fries, I snag your drink,
In these mad moments, our hearts sync.

Moments Crafted in Eternity

We're time travelers in thrift shop threads,
Find treasures in places where logic dreads.
Every tick-tock, we giggle and sigh,
Crafting wild dreams that teach us to fly.

With socks that clash and shoes untied,
We stroll through parks, with joy as our guide.
Every step screams, 'This life is a jest!'
In chaos and love, we are truly blessed.

Together We Paint the Sky

We throw colors like kids in a rain,
Giggles erupt over a bright pink stain.
You splash the blue, I dab on the green,
Our masterpiece glows in a world so serene.

Birds in the breeze dance to our tunes,
While our hearts beat loud under playful moons.
The clouds take shape, a dragon or cat,
In our laughter, we wear the world like a hat.

Echoes of Laughter and Love

We whisper secrets to the stars above,
Telling tales of mischief, chaos, and love.
With hearts of children, we run through the night,
Echoes of laughter turn dark into light.

You tickle my nose, I fumble my drink,
Lost in your gaze, I can't help but blink.
With silly confessions and reasons to cheer,
In this wild circus, you're my favorite peer.

Treasure Map to Happiness

With a treasure map in hand, we roam,
X marks the spot, where we call home.
Pirates of joy, with laughs as our gold,
Each giggle a gem, more precious than old.

We chart the course of silly delight,
Finding buried treasures both day and night.
With compasses spinning and hearts set free,
Every laugh is a step toward a grand jubilee.

Whispers in the Wind

The wind carries secrets, tickles my ear,
It whispers sweet nothings, oh so near.
Floating like feathers, on breezy highs,
We dance with the clouds, under blue skies.

Each gust is a giggle, a playful tease,
Turning mundane moments into such ease.
With every flurry, our spirits take flight,
Whispering dreams on a magical night.

A Tidal Wave of Love

Here comes the wave, splashing with glee,
Riding the surf, you and me.
Splashing and flopping, we giggle and scream,
Drowning our worries, like fish in a stream.

With salt on our skin and smiles so wide,
We catch every moment, like the best ride.
A tsunami of laughter, joy's perfect blend,
In waves of affection, there's no end.

Colors of Shared Dreams

With crayons of joy, we doodle our fate,
In the coloring book of love, there's no hate.
Each stroke a story, vivid and bright,
Painting our lives with pure delight.

Mixing our palettes, we splash and we play,
Every hue a memory, brightening the day.
From laughter to whispers, our canvas unfolds,
Creating a masterpiece, forever retold.

Harmonies of the Heart

In the kitchen, we dance so bold,
With spatulas as microphones, stories told.
Our pancake flip, a daring feat,
You laugh, I stumble, oh, isn't this sweet?

In mismatched socks, we stroll the street,
Avoiding puddles that threaten our feet.
A dance-off with strangers, a good show,
While squirrels judge us, they steal the show!

With your quirky jokes and my silly rhymes,
We weave through life, oh how it shines!
Each moment a giggle, each laugh a tease,
In our crazy world, we do as we please.

Unwritten Adventures

We chart our course on a crumpled map,
With no GPS, it's more fun to flap.
Each wrong turn leads to a cafe nook,
Where the barista smiles and we share a look.

Sailing the couch for a treasure chest,
With pillows for sails, we try our best.
The carpet turns ocean, our dog as the beast,
Sailing on whims, a whimsical feast!

On unmarked trails, we leap and stumble,
In the midst of chaos, we laugh and fumble.
Through mud and through rain, with hearts so wide,
Each unexpected turn is a thrilling ride!

Blossoming in Color

In a field of daisies, we paint with glee,
Your blue hair clashes with my bright green spree.
With splashes of paint, we create a mess,
And giggle at trees that wear our dress!

Pudding fights under the summer sun,
I throw, you duck, but we're still great fun.
Sticky fingers and laughter explode,
As we race to the hose for a cleansing code.

Under neon lights, our art comes alive,
In a pop-up gallery where dreams thrive.
Each piece a wink, a chuckle, a kiss,
Our love is a canvas, impossible to miss!

Fleeting Glances

In the coffee shop, our eyes collide,
You drop your muffin, it's quite the ride.
With crumbs on your face, I can't help but smile,
Our clumsy charm makes this moment worthwhile.

On the bus, we share awkward stares,
You pretend to read; oh, what a pair!
When you snort at my joke, the whole bus roars,
Our laughter echoes, breaking down doors.

In crowded rooms, it's a secret game,
A wink, a nod, but no one's to blame.
Each laugh and nudge builds a silent spree,
A tapestry woven just for you and me.

Endless Journeys

On forgotten roads, we wander and roam,
With snacks packed tight, our hearts call it home.
Each twist and turn brings a fresh surprise,
Like that squirrel who stole your fries!

In the backseat, you tell ghost stories,
While I mimic your woeful glories.
Traveling light with a suitcase so small,
Together we conquer, we have it all!

From city lights to the mountain peaks,
With each little stop, our friendship speaks.
Adventure awaits in the simplest thing,
With moments like these, oh, how we sing!

Rustling Leaves of Affection

In the breeze, your giggles sway,
Like rustling leaves on an autumn day.
You steal my fries with a cheeky grin,
In this dance of love, we both win.

Your socks mismatched, a colorful spree,
You claim it's fashion, but I just see
The fun in every quirky spark,
In your world, I'm the lark.

Moments Frozen in Time

Caught in a snapshot, you make a face,
I freeze it forever, 'till I find my place.
In the library, you laugh out loud,
Making people stare from the crowd.

Your stories bubble, like soda in spring,
With every word, my heart takes wing.
We chase the sunsets, quirky and bright,
In our little saga, everything's right.

Cusp of Forever

On the brink of the timeless fight,
You steal my bite of cake, all in delight.
Five-second rule, you toss it away,
In this crazy game, we both want to play.

With silly nicknames, we can't help but laugh,
Your clumsy dance, a comic paragraph.
We tiptoe on clouds, and skip on the ground,
In our silly love, pure joy is found.

A Dreamscape Shared

In our whimsical world where unicorns toast,
We juggle our dreams like a breakfast roast.
You chase rainbows, while I steal a nap,
In our vivid dreams, it's a wild mishap.

We laugh in colors, the skies turn pink,
Every shared moment makes my heart wink.
You're the punchline to my wandering whim,
Together we shine, on a whimsical trim.

The Sweetness of Our Story

In a world where socks don't match,
We dance to tunes that others scratch.
Honey drips from our tea, oh so sweet,
Every misstep makes our day complete.

You steal my fries, I munch your pie,
A game of love, oh me, oh my!
We giggle like kids, the world's our stage,
Writing our tale, page by page.

With coffee spills and laughter loud,
We climb our dreams, souls unbowed.
Chasing our whims like puppies in the park,
Finding joy in every little spark.

So here's our toast, a clumsy cheer,
To the sweet moments shared each year.
May our story hug us tight,
Like a blanket on a chilly night.

Starlit Promises

Underneath the sparkling skies,
We make wishes without goodbyes.
Your snoring's a symphony, it's true,
But I wouldn't trade it – I love you, too!

With ice cream drips and silly hats,
We plan our world, it's full of laughs.
Waltzing through puddles, splashing around,
Life's so much fun when love's all found.

We twirl like leaves caught in a breeze,
Cheesecake debates that leave us at ease.
Every secret giggle steals my breath,
With you, I dance like there's no death.

Let's paint the night with our hopes aglow,
In the wildest dreams, together we grow.
Hand in hand, let's leap through the stars,
Silly wishes, they're really ours!

Embracing Every Breath

With every hiccup and every sigh,
You're my favorite reason to fly.
We howl at the moon in delightful ways,
Laughing with echoes that stretch for days.

You trip on your laces, I burst out loud,
A tangle of limbs, we're quite the crowd.
Together we juggle dreams in the air,
With grins that show how much we care.

Every sneeze a symphony, heartfelt and true,
Life's perfect chaos, it's me and you.
From silly dances to snack-filled nights,
Each moment with you truly feels right.

So let's race clouds and chase down the sun,
In the game of our hearts, we've already won.
Bubbles and giggles, joy's our muse,
In this sweet embrace, we simply choose.

Kaleidoscope of Emotions

With shades of laughter and hues of delight,
We paint our world, oh what a sight!
From pancake fights to movie nights,
Every moment's a laugh, it just feels right.

You wear my shirt, I wear your grin,
In our twisted games, we always win.
Like kittens in boxes, it's unstructured play,
Chasing the sunsets, in a quirky way.

The ticking clock can't keep us still,
With adventures brewing, we sip and spill.
Our hearts a compass, leading the way,
To the epic tales we craft every day.

So here's to the mess, the winks and the cheer,
Together, adore, forever, my dear.
In this vibrant dance of life, let's twirl,
For joy is our anthem, in this crazy whirl.

Heartstrings of a Shared Tale

In a tangled web of socks we find,
Two hearts beating, forever intertwined.
With laughter echoing through the hall,
We juggle life, and sometimes fall.

Adventures start with coffee spills,
And dreams that pop like stubborn pills.
A dance-off in our mismatched shoes,
Making up rules as we choose to lose.

A Voyage of Endless Possibilities

Setting sail on a pizza slice,
Navigating through dreams, oh so nice.
With a map that's drawn in crayon red,
We create stories, then giggle instead.

The GPS lost, we roam like cats,
Ducking under tables, dodging chats.
A treasure found in the fridge's glow,
Pizza again? Oh yes, let's go!

Unity in Serenity

In our cozy chaos, we find delight,
Stumbling over pillows every night.
You steal my fries, I sip your drink,
Together spinning like a roller rink.

With each shared grin, our worries decrease,
A perfect blend of madness and peace.
Who needs a movie? We create our show,
Life's silly twists, the best way to grow.

The Sweetness of Now

There's icing on our silly cake,
With every joke, a giggle we make.
Sprinkling joy like confetti in air,
Oh, how we thrive on this silly affair!

From morning's toast to evening's tea,
The sweetness of now is just you and me.
With all our quirks, we're a splendid team,
In this wacky world, we'll forever beam.

A Journey through Sunlit Skies

We float on clouds with ice cream cones,
Sipping sunshine, trading groans.
The birds wear hats, oh what a sight,
As we giggle through our flight.

Chasing butterflies in polka dot socks,
Finding treasures in our mismatched blocks.
A bubble bath of clouds to dive,
With every splash, we come alive.

Pineapple umbrellas atop our drinks,
We dance a jig and have no links.
With every twirl, our laughter grows,
In this whimsical world, anything goes.

So let's soar high, on giddy bliss,
Hand in hand, count every miss.
For each wrong turn, we'll spin and sway,
In this silly, sunlit ballet.

Wrapped in Warmth

On chilly nights, we snuggle tight,
Wrapped in blankets, oh what a sight.
With popcorn fights and laughter loud,
We're the silliest duo in the crowd.

You steal the covers, I take the cheer,
Together we conquer, oh dear, oh dear!
With your goofy grin and my silly face,
Our love dances in this cozy space.

We build our world from marshmallow fluff,
In pillow forts, we talk tough.
With your snorts and my crazy jokes,
Our hearts beat loud like happy folks.

As morning breaks with golden light,
We find new games to start the fight.
With every hug, the warmth's sincere,
In this fuzzy love, there's nothing to fear.

Echoes of Laughter

In the park where we chase the breeze,
With bubble wands, we do as we please.
The squirrels laugh at our silly ways,
As we waltz through whimsical plays.

Each hiccup shared, a joyous sound,
Tickling ribs, joy knows no bound.
With walks on stilts or backward runs,
We find echoing joy in little funs.

The moon giggles at our midnight spree,
We dance like shadows, wild and free.
Under starlit skies, we softly sing,
In our laughter lies everything.

With every joke and playful tease,
We bind our souls with utmost ease.
This melody of giggles we spin,
In the echoes of laughter, we always win.

Dreams Woven in Twilight

When twilight whispers, soft and low,
We weave our dreams like a vibrant show.
With fireflies buzzing, stories unfold,
In the warmth of dusk, our hearts feel bold.

With silly faces and winked eyes,
We chart our course through cotton-puffed skies.
Every wish is sprinkled with stardust bright,
In this fabric of dreams, we take flight.

Cartwheeling into the sunset's glow,
With every hug, our spirits flow.
Costumed pigeons in a tapping dance,
In this twilight realm, we take our chance.

So come dear friend, let's sway and dive,
In this twilight where we come alive.
For in this playful, wild embrace,
We find our joy in every trace.

A Canvas of Wishes

In a world where time stands still,
We're painting laughs on every hill.
With brushes made of silly thoughts,
A masterpiece of joyful knots.

We'll splash some color, bright and bold,
Creating stories yet untold.
With every stroke, a giggle flows,
In our gallery, the fun just grows.

From clouds of whipped cream, we will soar,
Chasing dreams like kids in a store.
With hearts that dance like stood-up chairs,
Our laughter rings through the open airs.

So let's create our silly scheme,
Where everything's a happy dream.
In this world of whimsy's sway,
We'll make each moment a holiday.

Embracing the Infinite

In a universe of quirky quirks,
We find our way through all the jerks.
With you, the stars align just right,
A cosmic joke, a lovely sight.

We orbit round like planets do,
But no black holes can suck us through.
Your laughter is my guiding light,
We're swirling 'round, what a delight!

With every twirl, we make a scene,
Like socks that vanish in the machine.
In this wild dance of make-believe,
We'll spin and giggle; we won't leave.

So here's to our absurd parade,
In our infinite charade.
Together we create our fate,
A cosmos filled with love—just great!

Serenade of Shared Moments

Under the streetlight's golden glow,
We steal the show with every flow.
Two clowns on stage, we play our parts,
With twinkled eyes and goofy smarts.

Your jokes are puns that hit me right,
A tickle fight in the middle of night.
With every glance, my heart sings loud,
Together we stand, merry and proud.

From bread fights to our dance-off spree,
Each moment bursts with hilarity.
We'll serenade the moonlit skies,
With silly songs and crazy highs.

In this duet of crazy dreams,
We're woven tight; it's how it seems.
Through every laugh, our love will grow,
A symphony of joy and glow!

The Dance of Our Echoes

In a room where echoes play their tricks,
We twirl around, doing silly flicks.
Your laughter dances off the walls,
As we create our joyful calls.

With every step, we trip and sway,
Like unwritten rules in a ballet.
Our hearts collide in a clumsy beat,
Finding rhythm in our goofy feat.

In this carousel of whirling minds,
We leave behind what life unwinds.
Spinning tales of joy and glee,
Rhythms shared, just you and me.

So take my hand, let's laugh and spin,
In this dance of ours, let's dive within.
With every echo, our love's displayed,
In the joy of games that never fade.

Stars Aligning Quietly

In pajamas we dance, no need for the floor,
The fridge is our stage, who could ask for more?
Your laugh is the rhythm that guides all my moves,
As we twirl through our kitchen, the chaos approves.

We toast with our mugs, filled high to the brim,
At midnight we sing, while our neighbors look grim.
Like fireworks popping with every wild cheer,
In our cozy domain, the world disappears.

The Language of Us

You speak in emoji, I decode the flair,
Each wink is a message, hanging in the air.
We chat with our eyebrows, expressions run wild,
As if we're two kids, from the same magic filed.

When you trip over nothing, I can't help but cackle,
Your smile is electric, life's grandest sparkle.
We write our own script, no need for a play,
In a theater of laughter, we stay night and day.

Elysian Fields of Connection

We roam through the park, like ducks on parade,
Your wiggle's a dance, an unconventional craze.
The trees chuckle softly as squirrels take flight,
While the sun paints our shadows in hues of delight.

With snacks in our pockets, and jokes on our lips,
We launch into banter like seasoned pros' scripts.
Each moment with you feels like slipping on shoes,
That fit just right, maybe with a hint of blues.

Beyond the Ordinary

A fortress of blankets, our pillows in tow,
We conquer the couch in a glorious show.
Your side-eye is lethal, your giggle a guide,
In this realm of mischief, we happily bide.

When life streamers fall, as they tend to do,
We catch them with joy, crafting rainbows anew.
With snorts and with snickers, the day drifts away,
In the land of absurd, forever we'll play.

A Tapestry of Our Lives

In a world of mismatched socks,
We dance like chickens, moonwalk on clocks.
Spilling coffee, laughing wide,
You and I, the perfect ride.

With every stumble, laughter rings,
Building castles from our flings.
Elastic love, our silly spree,
Together we create a symphony.

Like spaghetti thrown against the wall,
Our moments stick, and oh, how we sprawl.
In every fumble, joy we find,
A masterpiece of the goofy kind.

Through the quirks, we share the sheen,
Our patchwork hearts, a vibrant screen.
Each thread a laugh, each knot a cheer,
In this crazy weave, love is near.

Hearts Unbound

Underneath a sky of pie,
We chase the clouds as they float by.
With rubber chickens in our hands,
We frolic through our wonderlands.

Like two clowns on a rollercoaster,
Every twist makes love a boaster.
With joy balloons and silly hats,
We juggle life, like playful cats.

In a bubble bath of giggles bright,
We serenade the moon at night.
Our hearts unbound, as wild as air,
Dancing like no one's watching there.

Through all the stumbles, bumps, and falls,
We build our life with joyful calls.
Each silly moment, pure delight,
We turn the dark into the light.

Celestial Conversations

Under stars with winking eyes,
We trade our truths and funny lies.
With ice cream cones and silly tongues,
Our universe in laughter hums.

Comets fly when we collide,
Our hearts a galaxy, open wide.
Like aliens with hearts aglow,
We explore this world, laugh and grow.

In our spaceship made of dreams,
We navigate love's crazy schemes.
With stardust sprinkled on our hair,
We chase the cosmos, without a care.

Each giggle lights the darkest night,
In celestial chatter, we take flight.
Our boundless hearts, a cosmic dance,
In every giggle, we find romance.

The Pulse of Our Union

Like a band with mismatched tunes,
We play our song beneath the moons.
Rhythms clash and harmonize,
Your laughter, my sweetest surprise.

In this carnival of goofy tricks,
We break the mold with silly kicks.
With every beat, our love expands,
A pulse of joy, with laughter's bands.

From wobbly bikes to silly pranks,
We conquer life with smiles and thanks.
Our hearts drum loud, a joyful sound,
Together, love's rhythm is profound.

Through every high and every low,
We find the groove where joy can flow.
In this dance of hearts, we spin,
Two crazy souls, forever grin.

Whispers of a Dreamscape

In a world where socks go missing,
I chase the cat, she's too dismissing.
Coffee spills like morning dew,
But laughter spills, and so do you.

We dance in rain, umbrellas fly,
A slipping trip, oh my, oh my!
With dreams that giggle in the night,
Our fun is bold, our spirits bright.

The fridge is bare, oh what a plight,
Yet pizza's here, it feels so right.
In this circus called our space,
Every clumsy step's pure grace.

So here's to laughter, cheers abound,
With every silly game we've found.
In this wild world, just us two,
We make the best, it's funny too!

Heartbeats in Harmony

Your snoring symphony, like a tune,
Wakes the sun, makes the morning swoon.
Pancakes flip like acrobats,
In the kitchen, we're worn-out cats.

Jogging together, what a sight,
Tripping over shoelaces tight.
We laugh as we dash, arms like wings,
Two dorks who feel like kings.

When life gives lemons, we make tart,
Chasing dreams with joyous heart.
With every quirk and every jest,
Together, we are simply blessed.

So here's to us, in our playful spree,
With love so wild, so crazy, so free.
Our hearts beat loud, can you hear the sound?
In our silly dance, we're joyfully bound!

Embracing Tomorrow's Light

We wake up late, oh what a blast,
Dancing in pajamas, having a feast fast.
With cereal rocks and milk streams,
We sparkle in our wacky dreams.

A trip to the store feels like a quest,
Arguing over what's the best.
You want the chips, but I want the cheese,
Who knew grocery fights could please?

Under the stars, we share moon pies,
In this wacky world, a huge surprise.
Your goofy laugh lights the night,
In your embrace, everything feels right.

Will tomorrow come with more of this cheer?
With you beside, I've nothing to fear.
So here's to giggles, the silly and bright,
In our oddball love, we find pure delight!

A Tapestry of Togetherness

Your dance moves, an incredible sight,
They resemble fish, with all their might.
In our living room, we twirl and spin,
With laughter echoing, let the fun begin.

Cupcakes explode in a frosting fight,
Who knew dessert could give such delight?
We wipe our faces, giggles prevail,
In this messy love, we never fail.

Pillow forts made, a castle grand,
Defending it from your sly hand.
The battle rages, yet love's our bond,
In this playful war, we're highly fond.

As the sun sets, we fade in tone,
But in our hearts, we've found a home.
So here's to each jest, each silly tease,
In our tapestry woven, we find our ease!

Unwritten Journeys of the Heart

We're two lost maps, folding in the breeze,
Writing stories with every silly tease.
Your laugh's a compass, pointing me right,
On this grand adventure, oh what a sight.

Every twist and turn, a laugh and a chase,
Caught in your smile, I find my place.
With snacks in the backseat, we drive for a while,
Through puddles and giggles, we conquer each mile.

Between the bumpers and the silly honks,
We dance to the rhythm of cereal box flanks.
A treasure map inked with ketchup and fries,
In this erratic journey, joy never lies.

So here's to our paths, yet to be drawn,
In the quiet of dusk, with the pink of the dawn.
No GPS needed, just you by my side,
Through this wacky life, in love we shall ride.

Embracing Every Color of Us

We paint our mornings in hues of delight,
With pancake rainbows, what a sweet sight.
Your quirky jokes, like splashes of red,
Stay close to my heart, like buttered toast spread.

In the gallery of quirky mishaps we dwell,
Where laughter can ring like a whimsical bell.
You spill your drink, I grin like a fool,
Our messy canvas, well, what a cool school!

Every mismatch creates a stroke so divine,
Like socks on the shelf, oh how they entwine.
We dance with our colors, bright as can be,
In this riot of laughter, just you and me.

So let's mix our shades, both wild and serene,
In the heart of chaos, you reign as my queen.
Life's palette is crazy, let's splash it around,
With you in my spectrum, pure joy's what I've found.

The Canvas of Our Dreams

With brushes in hand, we start our grand show,
Creating a world where imagination flows.
You toss paint like confetti, and I blend the tone,
Together we make art that feels like home.

Our easel's a stage, where colors collide,
With every stroke laughter, we take in our stride.
A splash of pure joy, a dab of surprise,
In this canvas of nonsense, our love surely flies.

The night falls around with stars up above,
We sketch out the dreams, the ones that we love.
With canvas so vivid, no need to erase,
In the gallery of life, we've found our place.

So let's drip and let splatter, let's twist the night,
Find solace in shades where everything's bright.
In our masterpiece made with whimsical cheer,
Every stroke whispers, "You're the one, my dear."

Stars Aligned in Love's Embrace

A little mishap, bumping heads in the dark,
We giggle and tumble, igniting a spark.
Under the cosmos, we trip on our feet,
Stargazing delight, our love is so sweet.

We map out the heavens with ice cream in hand,
Counting the wishes we drew in the sand.
Every wish throws stardust through the night air,
With your goofy grin, I'm beyond compare.

Your jokes are like comets, they fly and they zoom,
Turning dull nights into vibrant bloom.
We dance with the planets, and trip over dreams,
Chasing bright constellations and curious schemes.

In this universe built on laughter and cheer,
With you by my side, there's nothing to fear.
So let's chase the stars, let our hearts take a race,
In this silly world, we'll find our own space.

The Symphony of Togetherness

We dance in rhythm to cartoons at noon,
Singing off-key, like a silly raccoon.
With laundry on our heads, we jive and sway,
Making a mess in our own funny way.

Your laughter's the drum, my jokes are the flute,
We twirl like wild goofballs in a bright, funny suit.
The music of us fills the quirky skies,
Where every glance is a sweet surprise.

With pots for our instruments and chairs for the beat,
We'll play our strange symphony — oh, what a treat!
The echoes of joy will bounce off the walls,
As we take center stage in our makeshift halls.

In this madcap world, you're my favorite tune,
Orchestrating chaos beneath the full moon.
Together we'll laugh, so let the notes flow,
In this wacky duet, it's you I know!

Clouds of Hope

On lazy afternoons, we chase fluffy dreams,
   On cotton candy clouds, or so it seems.
   We tickle the sky, giggling all the way,
   With wishes that dance in a goofy ballet.

We build fluffy castles from marshmallow fluff,
   Wrapped in the antics of our silly stuff.
Rain may come pouring, but we'll hold our own,
With umbrellas made from fruit, it's clearly well-known.

Up in the sky, we're the jesters of fate,
Making rainbows with laughter, never too late.
We'll paint the horizon with colors so bright,
And nap on the clouds, till it's time for the night.

So let's sail our ships of imagination wide,
With humor as sails, there's no need to hide.
In these fluffy worlds, hand-in-hand we drift,
   With jokes on our lips, each moment a gift.

Rays of Joy

In sunlight's embrace, we dance like mad stars,
Twisting in shadows, hiking on Mars.
With ketchup on fries and laughter on roast,
Our moments of joy are what I love most.

You shine like the sun, my partner in glee,
Together we're awkward, yet perfectly free.
With each silly mishap, we double the fun,
Making light of the world as we bask in the sun.

The echoes of laughter bounce off the walls,
With every found treasure, our friendship enthralls.
We ride on the waves of our ticklish delight,
In this radiant world where everything's bright.

Through rays of mischief, we'll frolic and play,
Collecting sweet memories, come what may.
In this carnival life, let's dance till we drop,
With vague common sense, we'll never stop!

Building Castles in the Air

We gather our dreams with glitter and glue,
In castles of whimsy, just us two.
Constructing our visions, with a pinch of play,
In neon foundations, we'll giggle all day.

With laughter as bricks, we'll lay down the fun,
Our roof made of chocolate, oh what a run!
Windows of wonder, doors painted bright,
Every angle designed to make us ignite.

In gardens of candy, where jelly beans grow,
We'll sip fizzy drinks — a bubbly show.
With clouds for our ceilings, we find our own cheer,
As we build little dreams, losing all fear.

So here's to our castles, defying the norm,
In this whimsical world, let's dance and transform.
With giggles and dreams, we'll forever ascend,
In this |theater of laughter, where love has no end!

Finding Paradise in Each Other

You're my loony compass, my guide through the day,
In a planet of odd, we share our own way.
With socks on our hands and goggles in sight,
We build up our playground, both silly and bright.

Our laughter's the map to this curious land,
Where jellyfish dance and doggies can stand.
With foam in our hair and joy in our stride,
In this arcane paradise, we'll take a wild ride.

We dive on a whim into pools of delight,
Where sea cucumbers wear tiny bow ties.
In this charming utopia, we're free as can be,
With cheer and connivance, just you and me.

So hand in hand, let's explore our own dreams,
Navigating life through laughter's bright beams.
In this wonderful land, let's frolic and sway,
For paradise blooms in our quirky ballet.

Timeless Whispers of Togetherness.

In a world that spins and twirls,
We dance like silly squirrels.
You laugh and roll your eyes with glee,
While I try not to trip on my knee.

We share our secrets, oh so deep,
Like how you steal the covers in sleep.
Your quirky ways, a lovely spell,
A perfect mix, together we gel.

With every laugh we spill, it seems,
We build our life on crazy dreams.
You draw the sun, I'll paint the moon,
A wacky tune that ends too soon.

So here's to us, the jesters bright,
In our own sitcom, what a delight!
I'll trip and fall, you'll laugh and shine,
With timeless whispers, love's a fine line.

Chasing Stardust

We run through fields, barefoot and free,
Chasing stars, just you and me.
With arms wide open, we aim for the sky,
While I keep asking, 'Can you fly?'

You grab my hand, a twist and a turn,
A comet's tail, it makes me yearn.
Together we leap, like frogs in the night,
With laugh-out-loud jumps, what a sight!

We count the stars, or maybe just three,
You say, 'One's for you and the other for me!'
We crack up giggling, it's sheer delight,
With every wish, our hearts ignite.

So here we are, in this cosmic race,
With stardust glittered all over the place.
Chasing bright dreams with awkward grace,
In this wacky world, it's our special space.

Heartbeats in Harmony

With every thump, we sway and sway,
In this offbeat dance, we giggle and play.
You tap your feet, I twirl around,
Making music without a sound.

Your heartbeat's rhythm, a playful drum,
While I hum silly tunes, oh what fun!
This quirky symphony, we compose,
Two silly creatures, a sweet repose.

We serenade the moonlit skies,
With laughter echoing, the time just flies.
The stars join in, they flicker and beam,
As we create our own crazy dream.

In this waltz of life, we find our groove,
With every step, our spirits move.
In this clownish dance, oh what a spree,
Two heartbeats jiving in perfect harmony.

Whispers of Tomorrow

In a time machine made of dreams,
We sip our tea, and talk of schemes.
I propose we live upside down,
You chuckle loudly, 'You silly clown!'

We sketch the future with crayons bold,
Drawing kittens that dance, or so we're told.
With wild ideas and goofy flair,
We plot our lives with loving care.

You say, 'Tomorrow, let's fly a kite!'
I reply, 'But only if it's pink and bright!'
We'll paint the town with pastel stories,
Our quirky path bathed in glories.

So here's to us, the dream absurd,
With every laugh, our hearts are stirred.
In all these whispers, our love will grow,
As two bright stars in a cosmic show.

Dancing in the Moonlight

Under the stars, we prance and sway,
Tripping on shoes that just can't stay.
A penguin slide, a twirl so grand,
You laugh and shout, let's make a band!

We dodge the squirrels, they join the beat,
With wacky moves, we can't compete.
The moonlight glows, our shadows play,
As laughter rings, we dance away.

Your hair a mess, my feet are sore,
But still, we leap, come back for more!
With goofy grins, we steal the night,
In this mad waltz, all feels so right.

So let's embrace each silly chance,
And groove around in our wild dance.
With every spin, our joy we cast,
In moonlit fun, we'll never last!

The Ties that Bind

Silly arguments over socks and tea,
You say 'my way' and I say 'maybe'.
With every squabble, a chuckle slips,
As we navigate through life's wild scripts.

Our matching shirts, oh what a sight!
Like two bright peas in a wobbly flight.
You roll your eyes; I give a grin,
These quirky ties, where do I begin?

Through tangled thoughts and messy days,
We find our humor in all the daze.
Your snorts and giggles are music sweet,
In chaos, we dance to an offbeat beat.

So here's to us, the strange and bold,
With goofy love worth more than gold.
In every tie, a story spins,
In this crazy life, oh how it begins!

Notes of Nostalgia

Remember that time we blared our tunes,
In my rusty car, under bright balloons?
The windows down, we sang off-key,
While seagulls squawked like they owned the sea.

Our high school days, with late-night snacks,
Tales of prom dates and soda hacks.
You spilled the beans; I lost my cool,
Those silly slips were our golden rule.

With backed-up laughs and meme-filled texts,
We replay memories, what's coming next?
Your elbow nudges, a wink, a jest,
In our comic book, we're truly blessed.

So here's to the past, a merry ride,
With laughter echoing, our hearts collide.
In glorious notes, our tale we weave,
Every silly line, we shall believe!

The Heart's Milestones

From awkward glances to heart-shaped fries,
We've skipped past hurdles with sweet surprise.
With every blunder, our love grew strong,
Like a catchy tune that feels so wrong.

Remember the time you bought me a cat?
It coughed up fur; we laughed at that!
One milestone crossed, with giggles galore,
Two hearts united, who could ask for more?

So here's to the dates, and silly fall downs,
With belly laughs amidst silly frowns.
We'll dance through life, with quirks entwined,
Creating moments forever aligned.

With every heartbeat, a giggle shared,
In our own world, where no one's scared.
Each milestone passed is a joyful cheer,
For your goofy love is what I hold dear!

The Glow of Companionship

In a world where socks do clash,
We dance like fools, a dizzy bash.
Your laugh's a song, a joyful sound,
In this silly life, we're joyously bound.

With chocolate stains on every shirt,
We stumble on, our feet in dirt.
Each moment's bright, a comical sight,
In the glow of us, the world feels right.

We share our dreams with ice cream spills,
And chase the sun through hills and thrills.
Your wink ignites my goofy grin,
Together always, we both win.

Through every mess, we'll find our way,
With jokes and laughter, every day.
In this great scheme, we light the beam,
In the glow of us, we truly beam.

Singing Shadows of Us

In shadows cast by pizza trees,
We sing our tunes, with utmost ease.
You strum my heart like it's a game,
With each off-key note, I stake my claim.

We tap-dance on our leafy floor,
And giggle like we're six once more.
Your silly hat and wobbly grin,
Make every loss feel like a win.

As moonlight glints on glasses raised,
Our laughter rings, the night amazed.
With every step, mischief abounds,
In singing shadows, joy surrounds.

The night is young, our hearts set free,
We twirl like leaves on a raucous spree.
Together we laugh, forever we hum,
As shadows dance to a song of fun.

Odyssey of Togetherness

We set sail on our floating dream,
With peanut butter and jelly cream.
Our compass spins, yet we don't fret,
For every detour is a silly bet.

With seagulls squawking jokes on cue,
And treasure maps that point to stew,
We hoist the sails with a hearty cheer,
In our grand adventure, there's naught to fear.

Each wave we ride is a wobbly laugh,
A paddle's stroke in our crazy craft.
With every splash and playful tease,
In togetherness, we find our ease.

As time flows on like a river's stream,
We'll chart the course of our shared dream.
In this odyssey, so wild and fine,
With you by my side, it all aligns.

The Pulse of Spring

In springtime's burst, our laughter blooms,
  Like tiny daisies in crowded rooms.
  Your quirky dance makes flowers sway,
  And brightens up the cloudiest day.

With muddy shoes and playful splats,
  We leap like frogs, and tumble like cats.
  The sun's our stage, the sky's our song,
  In this season, we can't go wrong.

Each chirp and giggle, a vibrant beat,
  As we chase butterflies with dancing feet.
  With every bounce, our spirits lift,
  This springtime love is the greatest gift.

Through puddles big and petals small,
  Together we rise, we never fall.
  With you, my dear, the world's in sync,
  In the pulse of spring, we laugh and wink.

Mosaic of Bliss

In mismatched socks, we dance and twirl,
With pancakes stacked in a sugary swirl.
You laugh at my hair, a wild mane,
But in our chaos, we both feel sane.

We chase the cat while pretending to fly,
As birds eye us from a tree nearby.
Your snorts of joy are silly and bright,
In this mosaic, everything feels right.

We craft a fort from cushions galore,
And read fairy tales 'til our eyes can't explore.
The world outside fades, a distant hum,
Together we make our own kind of fun.

In our bickering over the TV show,
You steal the remote, and I play my woe.
Yet every small fight only adds to the flair,
Who knew that love could be this rare?

Journeys Beyond Imagining

On a couch expedition, we set our course,
With popcorn mighty, and soda, a force.
We sail through channels, oceans of dreams,
Falling off cushions, or so it seems.

We pack for trips to Mars and beyond,
With chips and dip, we form a bond.
Your space helmet's made from a colander,
But in your eyes, the stars shine even farther.

Each 'road trip' is nothing more than a snack,
With faces stuck in maps, how did we crack?
A wild detour to our fridge of delights,
Finding treasures hidden in midnight bites.

Back to bed we stumble, late and giddy,
With dreams of adventures, oh so witty.
In our little world, we wander with glee,
No need for the cosmos, just you and me!

The Symphony of Us

You whistle tunes only dogs can decode,
While I hum along to our own little ode.
In pots and pans, we make a sweet beat,
With laughter that dances on our two left feet.

Your quirky notes cause a melodic mess,
Yet somehow it all makes a joyful press.
We might trip over rhythm, a comic delight,
But in this duet, everything feels right.

We compose our lives like an offbeat line,
With misplayed chords, and a hint of wine.
Your laughter erupts on a flat note or two,
Yet every crescendo feels fresh and new.

In our silly concerts with no audience near,
The music of us is all we can hear.
In this playful symphony, hearts loudly cheer,
Together we craft a song that's sincere.

Chasing the Horizon

We run barefoot to where the sun meets the sea,
Drawing circles in the sand, just you and me.
With each crashing wave, our worries erase,
As we make goofy faces, setting the pace.

You can't find your shoes, and I've lost my hat,
But we wouldn't trade moments like this for a cat!
The horizon beckons as dusk starts to fall,
With ticklish sand and laughter, we have it all.

Chasing shadows, we leap like fish out of water,
Silly as children, free as a daughter.
With each sunset, our glances exchange,
The horizons we chase are a little deranged.

So here's to our journey, with every wild mile,
In waves of adventure, we make each other smile.
With hearts as our compass, we always know true,
Every path leads to happiness, me and you!

In the Garden of Us

In a garden where daisies tease,
We dance like children, float on the breeze.
You trip on your shoelace, give me a grin,
I swear my heart gives a spin!

With butterflies buzzing, we whistle a tune,
Chasing shadows 'neath the big yellow moon.
Planting our laughter, digging up glee,
Who knew gardening could be this free?

You'll never believe, we found a new flower,
Turns out it's just broccoli—oh, what a power!
We laugh till we cry, can't handle the plot,
Simultaneously thrilled, who knew you were hot?

In our quirky patch, where the giggles grow,
Let's water our joy and just let it flow.
Two peas in a pod, plus one little bug,
We bloom in this chaos, how snug is our hug!

Radiance of Togetherness

Under a sky painted like a big bowl of soup,
We whirl like confused penguins, a clumsy troop.
Your laughter's a light that chases the gloom,
Even the pigeons gather around our room.

Like toast that pops up, all burnt and brown,
We share our odd stories, wearing our crowns.
You hum tunes off-key, I join in a beat,
Together we make even nonsense sound sweet.

Side by side, we pick fruit from the tree,
You're a peach and I'm just a nutty decree.
Our moments like jelly — sticky yet bright,
We smile like kids sneaking candy at night.

With each silly mishap, our spirits will soar,
In this hilarious journey, there's always much more.
Chasing sunsets in flip-flops, that's our cue,
To celebrate this quirksome world, just us two!

The Art of Belonging

You and I are like socks that don't quite match,
A vibrant pair, who knew we'd hatch?
With splashes of color, and patterns askew,
We strut through life, that's our cue!

In a coffee shop brawl, I stole your last sip,
We played rock-paper-scissors, oh, what a trip!
You cheered at my dance moves, seriously so grand,
Who knew my chicken pose could ever be planned?

We can't draw worth beans, but we splash like pros,
Painting our days with outrageous shows.
Your quirks are a canvas, my canvas a hoot,
In this masterpiece life, we sprout funky roots.

Side by side, let's build a tall tower,
Out of pizza boxes, oh what a power!
In this wacky existence where laughter is key,
We're the strange artists that only we see!

Portraits of Joy

We snap goofy selfies, with faces that wobble,
Turning the mundane into a delightful gobble.
With winks and wild hair just like a mad clown,
Joy blooms like daisies in our goofy town.

On rainy days, we dance in the puddles,
Splatting our dreams, oh the gleeful cuddles!
You throw me a wink, I slip on a shoe,
Together we giggle, it's the best of our crew.

Like little kids in a field full of glee,
We chase playful rainbows, just you and me.
In our silly adventure, the world's our stage,
Each laugh we share ripples, page by page.

In this portrait of joy, we color outside,
With blobs of laughter, let's take a ride.
Through life's art gallery, so lively, so bright,
Where every misstep adds spark to our light!

Dancing on Cloud Nine

Bouncing on air like a jellybean,
Twisting together, a silly scene.
You laugh so hard, you snort a bit,
Every clumsy move feels like a hit.

Your two left feet found the rhythm right,
With every slip, we take flight.
In our own world, we sway and spin,
Who knew two dorks could have such a win?

Our giggles ring, like bells in spring,
Under the stars, we dance and sing.
Gravity's lost, it just can't hold,
In this crazy ride, we strike gold.

So here we are, just you and me,
A quirky duo, wild and free.
On cloud nine, we trip and twirl,
In this wacky love, we whirl and swirl.

The Melody of Us

Every note a little offbeat,
Yet somehow, it feels so sweet.
Your voice cracks like a chicken's squawk,
But we laugh and dance like a silly talk.

With pots and pans as our drumset,
Creating music, no hint of regret.
The neighbors peek with curious eyes,
As we strike a pose and improvise.

We duet like two cackling geese,
In our harmony, all worries cease.
Your off-key soul, my heart's delight,
Together, we shine, oh what a sight!

So let's compose our grandest tune,
Underneath a jiving moon.
In this cacophony, we choose to stay,
To make melodies in our funny way.

Fulfilling Fantasies in Twilight

As the sun dips low, we take a leap,
Into dreams, where secrets we keep.
Wishing on stars, our goofy aims,
Like riding unicorns in silly games.

Caught up in whims, we spin around,
In this twilight, we've truly found.
Giggling fairies play hide and seek,
In our fairy tale, no chance to be bleak.

With laughing dragons and pizza pies,
We frolic under cotton candy skies.
Imagination wild, hearts in flight,
In our dreamy world, nothing's a fright.

So join me, friend, in this brilliant mess,
Every moment just adds to our bliss.
Darkness can't catch us with its scheme,
As we live each sunset, chasing the beam.

Cherished Moments

With you, each day is a playful chase,
From breakfast spills to a wobbly race.
A tickle fight turns into a mess,
In our world, there's no need to stress.

Bumping into walls like we own the place,
Every little moment, we embrace.
Finding joy in a simple spoon,
Making laughter our daily tune.

The clock may tick, but we dance in time,
With each silly stunt, love feels sublime.
Here's to the giggles, to the ice cream spills,
In these cherished moments, our humor fills.

So let's compile our goofy tales,
With laughter echoing through the gales.
In this playful bond, let's always stay,
As we make more memories, come what may.

Endless Echoes

Through hallways echoing up to the moon,
We laugh so hard, the world's our tune.
Every joke, a boomerang in flight,
As echoes bounce back, day turns to night.

From whispered secrets to nonsense rhymes,
Creating a legacy through silly times.
In our echo chamber, joy multiplies,
As we dance shyly under starry skies.

Chasing the echoes that fill the air,
With every giggle, we banish despair.
In this rhythm of heartbeats shared,
Together we conquer, unprepared.

So let's turn the volume of laughter high,
In this symphony, we'll never say goodbye.
With you, my friend, forever we'll roam,
In echoes of love, we are always home.

Drenched in Affection

We dance in the rain, without any care,
Umbrellas all tangled, but we're a rare pair.
Your laughter erupts like a joyful surprise,
As raindrops do pirouettes off your bright eyes.

Splashing in puddles, we leap with great glee,
Wishing for mermaids to join in our spree.
You tug at my heart with your drenched little grin,
Our soggy escapades, where does fun begin?

Tales of Serendipity

Stumbling through life, we trip over fate,
You stole my taco, but oh, that's just great!
With every misstep, there's laughter to share,
Life's game of clumsiness, nothing can compare.

A hiccup. A tumble. A pint of ice cream,
You fall into my heart; it's a comic routine.
Fortune's odd twists lead us on this mad race,
Each wrinkle and giggle, a mark on our face.

Serenades of the Soul

You sing out of tune, but it's music to me,
A serenade crafted from love's clumsy spree.
With sock puppets jiving, and cookies that burn,
We croon to the moon, and to laughter we turn.

Dancing in kitchen, with flour as our snow,
You twirl like a dervish, your energy's glow.
The serenade plays, though the notes may be wrong,
In this quirky duet, we've found where we belong.

Nestled in Dreams

In pajamas adorned with bright cartoon flair,
We drift off to worlds where there's so much to share.
Dreams filled with tacos, and giant balloon fights,
With you by my side, every day is delight.

We wake up all tangled, a laughter-filled mess,
Your snore's like a chorus, but I must confess.
In the realm of sweet slumber, our spirits unite,
Each dream's a mischief—a marvelous flight.

Unfolding the Magic

In a land where socks disappear,
Dancing with shoes draws you near.
Jellybeans rain from the sky,
As we giggle, you and I.

Wizards that wear polka-dot ties,
Bake cakes that make us laugh and cry.
Chasing ducks on a skateboard ride,
Side by side, our worlds collide.

Balloons that float in the breeze,
Kites take flight with effortless ease.
A tap dance on a trampoline,
Joy rides in our wildest dream.

Spinning tales like cotton candy,
Every moment feels so dandy.
In this place of silly cheer,
Nothing can keep us from here.

Sails in the Breeze

With a boat made of crackers and cheese,
We sail on waves of fancy tease.
Riding tides of ice cream delight,
Under rainbows that glow so bright.

Fish in hats tell funny tales,
As we pilot the ship with flails.
Coconut crabs in tuxedos dance,
While seagulls join in our romance.

Our compass spins in circles grand,
Locating giggles across the sand.
Every sunset brings such delight,
As we chase the stars each night.

Laughter echoes across the sea,
In this world, it's just you and me.
With each wave, our hearts collide,
Sails in the breeze, our joyful ride.

When Hearts Sing

In a park where the squirrels wear hats,
We twirl and dance like acrobat cats.
With every leap, the clouds cheer loud,
Prancing around like a happy crowd.

Songs of laughter fill the air,
As we race through without a care.
Chasing pigeons with popcorn trails,
In this dream, there are no fails.

The sun winks as the flowers grin,
With petals that spin like a violin.
Our giggles rise like bubbles in flight,
Singing tunes that feel just right.

Moonlit nights and echoing chimes,
We create our own silly rhymes.
In this world of melody and fun,
Our hearts sing loud, forever young.

Secrets Beneath the Stars

Whispers float on the midnight air,
As constellations do their flair.
Dancing shadows with glimmering eyes,
Beneath the moon, no room for guise.

Cuddling close on a blanket spread,
With stories of gummy bears in bed.
Shooting stars with a wink and a nod,
Each wish made feels like a façade.

The crickets play their serenade,
As we share secrets never to fade.
In this cosmos of giggles and dreams,
Life is sweeter than it always seems.

Lost in the glow of twilight's breath,
Laughing at jokes that tease, not vex.
With every glance and silly sigh,
Beneath the stars, we soar so high.

Breathless in Your Aura

In a world of giggles, we dance today,
Your laughter's a melody, come what may.
Sticky ice cream, a chocolate-mustache show,
Chasing the squirrels, they run, oh so slow.

With every weird face, you're my favorite clown,
Strutting like peacocks, we won't wear a frown.
Jumping in puddles, splashing all around,
Who knew pure joy could be so profound?

We build our own castle, from pillows and sheets,
The Kingdom of Silly, where laughter repeats.
You spill the popcorn and we both just grin,
Silly adventures, where do I begin?

In this wild circus, you're the main act,
Balancing dreams, with a comic impact.
Breathless with joy, it's a wild rendezvous,
Every moment brighter, my heart belongs to you.

The Poetry of Together

You and I scribble on the walls of our heart,
With crayons of whimsy, let's make our own art.
Dancing in kitchens, the chef's hat askew,
Creating burnt toast, but it's perfect for two.

Whispering secrets in the night's cool embrace,
Your quirky little dance always sets the right pace.
With silly sock puppets putting on a show,
Each time we laugh, our love starts to grow.

In the land of the goofy, we build higher dreams,
Floating on wishes, like paper-cut beams.
We chase busy clouds as they merge and collide,
Two clowns in a circus, where joy is our guide.

With every small mishap, we celebrate life,
Turning the mundane into laughter rife.
In the poetry of us, no line goes unseen,
Together we're silly, a laugh machine.

Sunshine on Our Smiles

Like two rays of sunshine, we brighten the room,
Dancing in chaos, we banish the gloom.
Your quirky little giggle is my favorite sound,
In the circus of life, true joy we've found.

Building sandcastles with ice cream on top,
You trip on the waves, oh watch out, don't flop!
Splashing like dolphins, oh what a delight,
Bringing the fun, from morning to night.

Playing hopscotch on rainbows of glee,
Your silly remarks are a treasure to me.
Kites flying high, tangled just like our hair,
Every misstep is just part of our flair.

With sunshine on smiles, we conquer the day,
Your hand in mine makes it easy to play.
Together we twinkle, like stars in a race,
Finding joy in each moment, our own happy place.

Threads of Fate

Like yarn and a needle, we stitch up our dreams,
Through tangled adventures and whimsical schemes.
Your humor's the thread that weaves through the night,
With laughs as our fabric, everything feels right.

In a world made of marshmallows, we make our own path,
With plucky good cheer, some giggles, and laughs.
We'll dance with the moon, our feet light and free,
Making memories sweeter than honey from bees.

Life's a funny sitcom, we're stars in the play,
With each slip and trip, we'll just laugh it away.
Like two silly penguins, we waddle and slide,
Painting our journey with joy as our guide.

The tapestry of us, bright and unique,
With love as our fabric, we flourish and peek.
Threads of fate woven, in colors so bright,
Together we twinkle, a radiant sight.

www.ingramcontent.com/pod-product-compliance
Ingram Content Group UK Ltd.
Pitfield, Milton Keynes, MK11 3LW, UK
UKHW020107171224
452675UK00013B/1383

9 789908 012834